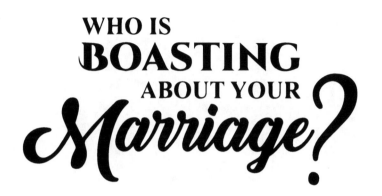

WHO IS BOASTING ABOUT YOUR Marriage?

NSEBOT IDOPISE IDO

authorHOUSE

AuthorHouse™
1663 Liberty Drive
Bloomington, IN 47403
www.authorhouse.com
Phone: 833-262-8899

Published by AuthorHouse 04/09/2021

ISBN: 978-1-6655-2246-5 (sc)
ISBN: 978-1-6655-2252-6 (e)

Library of Congress Control Number: 2021908465

Print information available on the last page.

CONTENTS

PRAISES

FOR PREVIOUS BOOKS BY THE AUTHOR

It is depressing indeed that both the ancient and modern society puts down the woman. For a widow who is faced with the stark reality of the loss of her husband, struggling to manage the sorrow and loneliness occasioned by her loss, the woman is further subjected to inhuman and degrading treatment that pokes at her personality. It is these acts of gender discrimination that Rev. Mrs. Ido seeks to address in her book "**BREAKING OUT AND WALKING TALL**".

She makes it known that this poor societal attitude is not in God's plan for the woman. She herein tells the woman that she has a purpose. She is not a "Plan B". She re-echoes the words of the master, "go and sin no more" thus:

"You have been offered a chance for a new beginning. You don't have to be anybody's chattel.

There is more to you than you are aware of.

Go and discover it.

Go and live it."

This book truly opens a new page for womanhood. It has blessed my life greatly which is why I didn't keep it but promptly shared it with a friend after reading it. It has made me to break out and I am now walking tall.

Ekaette Akpanabiatu
Daughter of the KING.

The first time I came across Rev. (Mrs.) Ido's book **"BREAKING OUT AND WALKING TALL"**, it was so captivating that I finished the entire seven chapters at a sitting and could not agree more with her thoughts on womanhood.

Interactions with her reveal that she does not only seek to help women discover themselves and be the best they can be; she also 'walks the talk'.

Mrs. Uduak Ekanem
Retired Director of Administration/ Gender Focal Person

Many human-abusers give lame excuses for marginalization, be it against children, women or humanity as a whole. Some blame it on cultural disposition, societal disvalue, religious beliefs, etc.

More so, it is disheartening when the Bible is used to back up this disdain.

In this book, **"BREAKING OUT AND WALKING TALL"**, the author, Nsebot Idopise Ido explains beyond culture, society, and religion, the irreplaceable value and God-ordained place of women, using scriptural truths. This book awakens the women without neglecting the men. I strongly recommend this book to all.

Rev. Dr. Iniobong F. Udoh
Chaplain, Victory Chapel
University of Uyo, Uyo,
Akwa Ibom State, Nigeria

The word that best describes the book "**BREAKING OUT AND WALKING TALL**" for me is; "*UNPUTDOWNABLE*".

Nathaniel Olayode
Minister at Faith Baptist Church, Oron
Nigerian Baptist Convention

I deeply appreciate the issues of mothering, leadership and womanhood raised in the book "**BREAKING OUT AND WALKING TALL**". It is frank, motivating and inspirational. I consider it a 'must read' for every woman, mother, daughter, in-law, grandchild and the husbands who marry and father those women.

Prof. Enoidem B. Usoro
DVC Academic
University of Uyo.

"**PUSH BACK YOUR FEARS**" is a wonderful capsule of crystal exposition of the emptiness of fear. Mrs. Ido has poured her scientific mind into this book with clear and empirical description in a very conversational style, as a mentor.

"**PUSH BACK YOUR FEARS**" is a tour into the dark dungeon of fear with the author as the tour guide shining the light into the dark crevices and exposing the nakedness and emptiness of fear coming down to give credence to the fact that fear is actually False Expectations Appearing Real.

The real-life application in all spheres of life and human endeavors makes the Bible come alive and is very commendable.

If you are experiencing fear in any form at any point in your life, this book is highly recommended. You won't be able to drop it, until you're through. It's a must read. I have been blessed by it.

Albert Udoh
CEO/Chief Business Architect, Entafrique Consulting Ltd.
Abuja.

The book "**PUSH BACK YOUR FEARS**" is very enlightening to every Christian looking to grow their faith. In a world of uncertainties, an age filled with almost the worst surprises, fear tends to creep into the heart. I therefore recommend the reading of this book to everyone and especially the Christian for growth and stability.

Prof Enoidem B. Usoro
DVC Academic
University of Uyo

As a colleague I know Mrs. Nsebot Ido, to be an authentic, sincere, humble servant of the highest God. A wife, mother, friend and sister. As God's warrior princess, she has diagnosed fear and has dispensed practical steps to push forward in the midst of it all. She is truly living the faith Walk in this book. Her book, "**PUSH BACK YOUR FEARS**", contains the keys you need for an exciting and fulfilling faith work and walk in God. It has been a tremendous blessing to me and to the many people I have recommended to read. I wholeheartedly recommend this book to every soul out there.

Pharm. Iniobong Josiah
Certified Family Life Coach, Trainer, Speaker
and Teacher at the John Maxwell Team.

The danger of not dealing with fear is not just in its effects, but also in its company. In the company of fear, we find doubt, discouragement, deception, despair, depression, etc. and ultimately death. Fear is a spirit that opposes our faith in God, and seeks to turn man's attention away from God. But as one noted: "fear knocked, faith opened, and no one was there. Nsebot Idopise Ido uses "**PUSH BACK YOUR FEARS**" to educate its readers how faith can respond to fear, and comprehensively do away with her effects and company.

I strongly recommend this book for everyone that desires an intimate daily walk with God devoid of fear.

Rev. Dr. Iniobong F. Udoh
Chaplain, Victory Chapel
University of Uyo, Uyo, Akwa Ibom State,
Nigeria

DEDICATION

This book is dedicated to my parents-in-law, Senor Elder Willie Ido (late), and Madam Grace Willie Ido popularly called Mma-Mma. Thank you for modelling for us a Christ-centered marriage.

ACKNOWLEDGEMENTS

I would like to use this medium to acknowledge and appreciate individuals and corporate bodies who have been instrumental to the making of this book.

I appreciate my husband of thirty-nine years – we are not counting because there is no need. We came into this union knowing that it shall be permanent. Through the years we have weathered many a storm and I know that it is only death that can part us.

The second slot goes to my church pastor, Rev. Ben Nkwocha. Much of the material in the book is from a sermon he graciously allowed me to preach at the wedding of one of our pastors. His wholehearted endorsement of that sermon encouraged me to ensure that the message does not die by putting it into print.

Also worthy of mention is Faith Onyedikachi (aka man of faith). He made sure I had a functional laptop at all times and never felt inconvenienced any time I called on him for help, considering my level of computer literacy.

Rev. Ezekiel Atang graciously agreed to do the foreword. Eventually he did more than write a foreword, he penned an endorsement. God bless you sir.

I must appreciate the members of Victory Baptist

Church, Ibeno for sharing their lives, burdens, successes and failures with me. It has contributed to some insights shared here.

Otobong Charles, my sounding board, with wisdom beyond his years has been of immense help in the editorial work and final packaging

Let me not forget my cheerleaders – Mkpouto, Ifiok, Imo and Udeme – the four daughters that prophesy in songs. They are always the first to proofread the manuscripts.

I return all the glory to God for the challenge to put this writing talent to use. It has proved to be a surprise to many who have known me closely for years without knowing this part of me. One recently endorsed this work with words which I believe you would love to hear so I quote:

> *A very well written biblical, anecdotal and practical book on Marriage. Clearly written by one who has lived and experienced the benefits of applying Biblical principles in handling the challenging issues of marriage. It covered most important topics including learning to accept your spouse as human and for who they are, cultivating mutual respect for one another out of reverence for the Lord Jesus Christ and making room for the individual identity of each spouse. The author without being preachy brilliantly interweaves foundational biblical principles along with practical and prescriptive advice for the couple desirous and willing to do the necessary work in their marriage of a lifetime. The book*

contains in-depth discussion of principles and practical steps on the subject of Sex and indeed "Making Love", done brilliantly with wit and humor in a way that would be beneficial across the broad age spectrum of married couples. Managing in-laws, an important aspect of a successful marriage was covered clearly and practically that the discerning couple would do well to learn from. The book concludes by using the metaphor of "the icing on a cake" to address the presence or the lack of children in a marriage in a very balanced way.

Overall, the book is very readable and the writing flows effortlessly in a way that every reader would be drawn to finish reading it at a siting.

- Nosayaba Evbuomwan, PhD

All scriptural quotations are from the New King James Version (NKJV) OF THE Bible unless otherwise indicated.

I accept full responsibility for any shortcoming or error in the final production and tender my unreserved apologies.

Shalom.

Nsebot Ido.

FOREWORD

I have read and done the foreword for quite a number of books on marriage and relationship, and I find this one quite satisfying. The reason is that it has been authored by a veteran in the practice of marriage according to the Bible. The Bible has a few marriage teachers, chief of whom were Paul and Peter. Paul taught by revelation, while Peter taught by experience, and they both did a fantastic job at it. It is okay, therefore, to teach marriage from the revelation stand point, but it is far much better to teach it from both angles and this writer does just that.

I sat under a very strong marriage teacher and counselor for fifteen years and during those years I really drank into the understanding of marriage and marriage operations according to the Bible. Little wonder then that few months after I got married, the Holy Spirit began to impress on me not only to begin to teach marriage, but to accept it as my main focus in life and ministry.

However, I taught more from revelation, with little or no experience whatsoever. Later down the road into my marriage, I had to obey and practice all the revelations I had taught. And I realized it wasn't that easy at all. It was really hard, but I could not argue with the facts and truths that had gone out of my mouth earlier. Those teachings of mine really shaped and are still shaping my marriage till this day. I consider myself really blessed of God to have encountered all that beautiful wisdom from God even without the benefit of experience.

I said all these to point out the fact that the author, Mrs. Ido has waited and waded into the experience of marriage for decades, guided by the word of God; and today she teaches from a very authoritative stand point. And here are my reasons:

- Many who have been married for as long as the author has been, would want to skew the teaching of marriage to fit into the narrative of their failures or successes but she has held on to the pure truth of God's word as it relates to marriage without compromise. And this includes those aspects of the word that are not comfortable in any way. It is not easy to find elderly married believers on the female side of the spectrum who still hold on to the simplicity of God's word, particularly as it affects submission and the like. This gives me great joy and hope indeed, and makes her not just worth reading, but worth following as well.

- Secondly, I have not seen any attacks on the men folk as some female marriage counselors would do. Rather, she has offered balance and wisdom to today's husbands. She has proficiently killed some painful arguments by offering counsel from the word of God; her personal experiences; as well as her balanced opinions. This I find very good and helpful. You will need to read this material to see my point. I find her a great breath of fresh air in the marriage discourse. As they say, she's been there, done that and came out affirming the word of God to be true. She didn't spare the foolishness of husbands, but she offered great help to them alongside chastening.

- She did not shy away from the tough subjects. I am referring to topics like marital sex. I personally did not expect her to venture into that area. I thought that the old school believers would rather avoid or ignore the sex talk altogether, but not this author. She has proven that there is nothing old school about sex and love-making in marriage. "Make love while having sex" is one of my take-aways on this subject. "While sex comes naturally, love making is a learning process". Very aptly put. The matter does not end there, it goes on to address sex in marriage at various ages in the life of the married couple. There is so much to glean from there.

Let me wrap up my appendage by making reference to her very last but so brief chapter. There she said, and I quote:

> *"When we are conscious of the fact that our marriages are speaking of Christ and the church, we will use every resource from the heavenly manual to make them speak well".*

In times past when poverty was the order of the day, the church evangelized with the promise of prosperity. We would say things like "come to Jesus and He will heal and prosper you" – even when the preacher was in poverty. We did so because the world was in so much need of financial blessings. But in the present age, the work is in so much command of finances, as such we can't successfully use it as promise or bait to bring certain people to Jesus anymore. There are greater needs in our time. There is a need for uprightness and character rectitude, and the world is hungry for it. The church happens to be the only solution for this need. The very best way we can cause the world to really hunger for God would be the peace, harmony and success of our homes. The rich are in bewilderment as to how to make their marriages work. Celebrities fall in and out of marriage as quickly as a person goes to bed and rises up again. There is obviously a very huge societal challenge in the area of marriage. And the success of a Christian neighbor's marriage will speak volumes to an unbeliever counterpart. It would make them ask questions and the believer will be able to showcase Jesus as the answer and by so doing fill up the kingdom of God.

It is for the foregoing that I make the following conclusions about this book:

i.   The author knows exactly what she is saying. She has the years under her belt, and her knowledge of the word of God is very balanced and accurate.

ii. This book will clear all forms of confusion regarding the marriage discourse. She has not left any shadows regarding all the issues she has brought up.

iii. It is a very suitable material for those about to wed, the just wedded and those who have been married for "donkey years". It will suit all categories of people, including the marriage counselor.

iv. It is a scholarly work as it has been well referenced. Several works and authors have been quoted here. Such respect for the opinion of other teachers in this subject has made it a material to respect and that can be trusted.

v. It is based on sound biblical doctrine.

vi. It is not misleading, extreme, or one-sided. It is without any form of bias for any gender. It is sound and solid. It has thrown so much light into some seemingly hard scriptures.

vii. The grammar is easy and comprehensible. The author obviously has a very good command of grammar, but did not burden us with too many complicated English words. That shows that her motive is to help us achieve understanding.

viii. I recommend this book to the clergy, bible schools and counselors who really want to be a blessing to the world of marriage and married people.

And to the author, I thank you on behalf of the body of Christ for adding your rich wealth of experience, both in marriage and scripture to the arsenal of knowledge already existent. We honor and appreciate you.

Pastors Ezekiel Atang
Lead Pastor, God's House of Refuge.
Marriage teacher and counselor.

INTRODUCTION

The assertion that marriage is a paradox in which, while some are rushing to enter others are working hard to exit is becoming increasingly true. While this adage attracted guffaws of mirth whenever it was rehearsed some years ago – mostly at bachelors' eve ceremonies – these days a thoughtful silence seems to overtake any audience in which the sentiment is touted. This reaction is not unconnected with the increasing rate of separation and divorce in society. Africa seems to have been spared somewhat since traditional values are still largely upheld maybe because we are "underdeveloped". As the light of development (so called) seems to dawn, we also seem to be in a hurry to catch up with our western cousins whose divorce rates are not just unflattering, but alarming. "…About 50 to 60% of married couples in the United States end in divorce. The divorce rate for subsequent marriages is even higher" (Adapted from the Encyclopedia of Psychology). The church has not been spared and the clergy seems to be taking the lead. There seems to be an increasing level of spousal intolerance which has divorce lawyers smiling to the banks at the expense of broken lives and homes. Even where the marriage is sustained, many couples endure their marriage situations for various reasons. These reasons range from the fear of what people will say, to what will happen to the children, to a desire to do that which is right in the sight of God. Spousal battering which may be physical, emotional or material is commonplace. It would be difficult to get correct statistics because many cases go unreported due to the fact that we are in an environment where people still feel it is a shame to take their marital problems outside of their home. As a result, many Christians hide their hurts and pain with a grimace while mouthing the religious mantra "It Is Well'. Still others play the ostrich. They pretend not to see the evil going on even when they could lend a helping hand.

However, we thank God for the light we see at the end of this tunnel of marital dis-ease. There is a little more enlightenment, with more married people ready to speak honestly and more pastors and churches gradually removing the mask that covered decay in marital relationships. It is heartening to read treatises like the one written by a young friend on their wedding anniversary:

> *"In marriage, you don't seek self*
> *You think the other more*
> *In marriage, you don't dream*
> *You leave fantasy to face reality*
> *Marriage is not for those who seek impression*
> *Marriage is for those who are ready to impact*
> *The house of marriage is not built on lies*
> *Her foundation must be true*
> *Many would want her like bed of roses*

But every rose bears thorns – (don't you know?)
The beauty of marriage is weird
Only a few understand the secrets
Love is not love if it cannot survive marriage
If you think you love, marriage will prove it
Fake fire burns ice – the real one flames
The home of marriage is in true hearts
Where trust, transparency, respect, loyalty
Faithfulness, love and care reside
Your fleet of cars, mansion, money means
NOTHING if you lack these spices
You must tame your greed to think of marriage
She is more satisfying than other treasures…"

(Udeme Inyang on Facebook
21st June, 2019).

Marriage is by its very nature a very unique and special school. It is the only school where the certificate is obtained at the point of entry, not at graduation. It is the only school that offers a joint certificate. In this school, only one of the joint owners of the certificate is likely to attend the graduation ceremony on this side of eternity and the said party will not be smiling or dancing. There might be drum rolls on that day of graduation but not for the merriment of the one that is left behind. There is only one textbook in this school and that is the Bible. Every other book written on or about it only serves as reference material. There is only one lecturer – the Holy Spirit – even though you may take tutorials from mentors. Marriage is made in heaven but lived only and solely on earth.

God who does all things beautifully designed marriage to showcase the mystic union between Christ and the church. As Apostle Paul so succinctly put it: *"For this reason a man shall leave his father and mother and be joined to his wife, and the two shall become one flesh." THIS IS A GREAT MYSTERY, BUT I SPEAK CONCERNING CHRIST AND THE CHURCH"*. (Ephesians 5:31-32 NKJV). Just as God looked at His creation and expressed His satisfaction with His handiwork as the Bible says, *"Then God saw everything that He had made, and indeed it was very good"* – Gen. 1:31 NKJV, so God intended to look at the institution of marriage, nod with satisfaction and say, "I speak of Christ and the Church". Much of the misconceptions and misunderstandings about the church of Jesus Christ on earth would automatically find their answers in the marriage relationship. However, the Devil, that old slue-foot who hates man with a perfect hatred, and tries to counterfeit, denigrate and deface every good thing that God does, would want to bring this school to disrepute so that he can hold it up to God with disdain and say: "I speak of Christ and the Church". That was the ruse he used when he attempted to challenge Job's commitment to God.

> *"Now there was a day when the sons of God came to present themselves before the Lord, and Satan also came among them.*

And the Lord said to Satan, "From where do you come?" So, Satan answered the Lord and said, "From going to and fro on the earth, and from walking back and forth on it. " Then the Lord said to Satan, "Have you considered My servant Job, that there is none like him on the earth, a blameless and upright man, one who fears God and shuns evil?" So, Satan answered the Lord and said, "Does Job fear God for nothing? Have you not made a hedge around him, around his household, and around all that he has on every side? You have blessed the work of his hands, and his possessions have increased in the land. But now, stretch out Your hand and touch all that he has, and he will surely curse You to Your face!" (Job 1:6-11 NKJV).

Of course, when we look at the church today, we see a lot of schisms with the fault lines falling along denominational, ethnic, doctrinal and even social divides. This is a reflection of what goes on in families. The general attitude towards marriage is more like that of a business contract in which the partners easily get fed up and call it quits regardless of who is affected. Most of the time it is the hapless children who never made a choice to be born but came by the will of this same intolerant pair, that are most affected. Regardless of the age of the children and how long they have witnessed the fragmentation of their parents' relationship, they still hope and pray that things will work out and they would live peacefully and happily together. Their desire for their parents' marriage is that "It shall be permanent".

Some try remarrying in the hope that they would get it right the second time where they failed the first time. However, most experiences of second or third marriages are like the ones described here:

> "I've been married three times, and each time, it was wonderful before we got married, but somehow after the wedding it all fell apart. All the love I thought I had for her and the love she seemed to have for me evaporated. I don't understand it" (The Five Love Languages, p.11).

It is against this background that God's people in all ages must contend for the sanctity of the marriage institution and strive to build an enviable family environment. This book is a contribution to the achievement of this idyll. It cannot address every marital issue but it will certainly set us on the path of ensuring that God, and not the Devil will be the one saying concerning our marriages: "I speak of Christ and the Church". When men and women begin to see their marriages as speaking of Christ and the Church, their attitudes will change. Marriage was meant to work. The manufacturer has left a comprehensive roadmap to help each couple navigating this terrain to make it safely to port.

I have had so much challenge writing this book that I am sure the kingdom of darkness is afraid of letting it come out. I have heard of writer's block but this time I have experienced it firsthand. It is with great passion and determination that I trudge on, knowing that the Lord has something to say through this His servant, made worthy only by the grace of the Lord Jesus Christ.

As you listen to His voice, I say to you concerning your marriage, "It shall be permanent". I understand that some reading this book are in marriage relationships that are not the best. In fact, they feel that "it shall be permanent" feels more like a life sentence without hope of parole than a benediction. Just hold on, read to the end, receive grace to obey the voice of the Lord. You will be glad you did. May you really be blessed.

CHAPTER ONE

Ultimate Satisfaction

Oh, satisfy us early with Your mercy,
That we may rejoice and be glad all our days!
Make us glad according to the days in
which You have afflicted us,
The years in which we have seen evil.

- Ps 90:14-15 NKJV

Many enter into marriage with wrong expectations and faulty motives. Some get married because of different kinds of pressure. These include age, parental pressure, peer group pressure, the desire to conform or the perceived inability to stay alone. Many women get married in order to escape the poor economy at their home of origin while some men get married because they need help with cooking, washing and other aspects of housekeeping. They expect their satisfaction to come when their spouse meets these needs. That is why they get easily disappointed when their spouses fail to live up to their expectations.

Women are especially prone to pressure arising from advancing age. The biological clock is ticking away and the optimal age for childbearing seems to be slipping out of their fingers. Meanwhile their peers, younger siblings, students and even nieces are getting married and giving birth. They are tired of being the universal auntie. The temptation is to get married to the next available man and manage as best they can. They feel their ultimate satisfaction is in getting married regardless of the moral, religious and spiritual antecedents of the prospective spouse.

For others yet, their motivation is the satisfaction of parental expectations. This pressure is felt by only-children maybe more than children who have siblings and maybe by sons more than daughters. Many fathers feel that if their sons do not marry and produce legitimate heirs their name might soon become extinct. Africa has her fair share of this mindset but it certainly did not originate with us. Abram had and expressed these same fears to God:

> *"But Abram said, "Lord God, what will You give me, seeing I go childless, and the heir of my house is Eliezer of Damascus?" Then Abram said, "Look, You have given me no offspring; indeed one born in my house is my heir!"*

> *- Gen 15:2-3 NKJV.*

Those who think this way do not understand that it is only one name that will outlast all names and that is the name of Jesus. As a matter of fact, when one has left this world as all one day will, he has no power over what is done with his name. Some even have the misfortune of seeing their names dragged in the mud during their lifetime. If you see Eli the priest, ask him. Even the sons of Samuel the great prophet did not follow his footprints. Solomon the preacher saw this as vanity and expressed same thus:

> *"Yea, I hated all my labor which I had taken under the sun: because I should leave it unto the man that shall be after me. And who knoweth whether he shall be a wise man or a fool? yet shall he have rule over all my labour wherein I have laboured, and wherein I have shewed myself wise under the sun. This is also vanity."*

> *- Eccl.2:18-19 KJV*

Others get married because of peer group pressure. While growing up you may have belonged to a group (didn't we all?) where you aired your plans and purposes and kept tabs on each other to see how far your dreams and plans are playing out. As each member of the group gets married, there is a loud, though often unspoken "who will be the next". Apart from the "who will be the next" there is also the unwritten desire to outdo the last one in the preparation, the train, the food, the souvenirs, the guests, the ceremony – both traditional and "white". This happens so much so that many get into debts they will spend their first few years of marriage trying to pay. They feel they will be satisfied if they have a wedding that is the talk of the town. Little do they realize that the wedding does not the marriage make. Many spend much time, effort and resources to make the wedding – a one day affair – "just so", whereas the marriage – a lifetime engagement – is hardly given a thought in terms of preparation.

There is also pressure based on the desire to conform to societal norms and values. The marriage ceremony must go through the full process: the traditional, the court and the "white". Many do not bother to think on the significance of these steps or see how they could collapse some steps to make it easier on the would-be spouse, family and friends. Many have lost potentially good relationships because of the desire to conform. It is important to note that having a white wedding does not make a marriage white. We have heard of people who left the beds of their lovers to get ready for their "white" wedding. Marrying in church does not necessarily make a marriage Christian. Today we have churches who will conduct wedding ceremonies for a fee. They even advertise this each time a wedding is conducted in their organization. They do not ask too many questions. There is little or no pre-marital counselling. They don't have to pastor either the bride or the groom. All you need to do is pay the prescribed fee and your satisfaction will be guaranteed. Though this is saddening, the practice seems to be gaining ground.

Many get married because they are scared to be alone. For these people, even when there are indications that the relationship is not the best it could be, they settle for second best because the alternative is staying alone, a situation they think they cannot cope with. (The Rules of Love –Richard Templar p.8).

The point needs to be made therefore, that ultimate satisfaction in all marriage issues is vested in God. He is the originator and sustainer of marriage. "In the United states couples that are marrying for the first time have approximately a 50% chance of divorcing. Psychologists are helping couples' "I do" last a lifetime through development and application of scientifically tested education programs." (www.apa.org accessed on 26/02/2019). As laudable as this initiative is, it will ultimately fail in bringing satisfaction if not predicated on the principles of God and His Word. The reason is simple: Marriage was God's idea from inception. It is He who saw the loneliness and aloneness of Adam and said, *"It is not good that man should be alone; I will make him a helper comparable to him."* – Gen 2:18 NKJV. As has been said again and again, "A marriage without God is a failed marriage". In order to find satisfaction in marriage therefore, an individual must first find satisfaction in God. There is need for a vibrant, current relationship with God that transcends the allegiance you have to your spouse. If one relates well with God, there is no way they can fail to relate well with their spouse. If your expectations of your spouse fail, your allegiance to, and satisfaction in God will enable you to continue loving him/her even when they don't deserve it. Forgiveness will be possible even if not easy when you remember how God, in Christ forgave you. When you find your ultimate satisfaction in God, you will understand that even when your spouse is going wrong you can get into the salvaging mode and on your knees draw him/her out of the fires of hell, the clutches of the strange woman or the self-destroying path of greed.

Often when one talks of satisfaction, it is easy to envisage a utopia where all is well, every need is met before it is even articulated and even wants are catered for. In marriage a woman may think that satisfaction is in marrying a man who is tall, dark, handsome and rich. For others, he must be articulate, speak English without a perceptible accent and of course his mother must be late. For the man, his satisfaction may be in finding a woman who is beautiful, tall, with all the curves at the right places, sophisticated and having a good job or business. "In this season of economic downturn, a non-working wife is a liability. It is necessary to marry a viable wife" – they say. Others think they will be satisfied if they marry a woman who is domesticated. She cooks, cleans, goes to market and is generally hard-working and non-complaining. She must not use make-up and must not like expensive things. She must be able to manage the scarce resources he is able to bring.

While it is good to know and articulate the virtues and characteristics one expects in your spouse-to-be, it is necessary to caution that those things that look like virtues today may turn to be vices some days hence. Also, human beings are changeable and greed can be masked when there is no means of expression. Where there is a vibrant relationship with God, there is rest that enables one to love the one he has married, warts and all.

What do we mean by a vibrant relationship with God? It means first of all that you are born again. You have appropriated the sacrifice of Jesus on the cross by which you have passed out from under the curse and have entered into the blessings of Abraham, whom God blessed in all things. It means that you take your spiritual exercises more serious than the athlete takes his training. It means learning to apply the word of God to every area of your life and more especially all aspects of the marriage relationship. Your commitment to Bible study, prayer, fasting, evangelism and stewardship must be exemplary. The praying person is a peaceful person. No matter how difficult the situation one faces, when he commits it to God he enters into rest. How do you commit your situation to God when you do not know His word? God is not honor bound to answer your prayers. He is honor bound to keep His word. How much of your prayers receive God's answers is dependent on how much of His word is in your prayers.

> *'Then the Lord said to me, "You have seen well, for I am ready to perform My word."'*
> *Jer.1:12 NKJV*

> *Also: "Hear, O Israel: The Lord our God, the Lord is one. Love the Lord your God with all your heart and with all your soul and with all your strength. These commandments that I give you today are to be upon your hearts. Impress them on your children. Talk about them when you sit at home and when you walk along the road, when you lie down and when you get up. Tie them as symbols on your hands and bind them on your foreheads. Write them on the doorframes of your houses and on your gates." Deut 6:4-9 NIV*

This sounds to me like the hallmark of vibrancy in one's relationship with God. No wonder He gave it as an instruction to the Israelites. A vibrant relationship with God releases the man to love his spouse as Christ loves the church and releases the woman to love honor and obey her spouse as the church does to the Lord.

CHAPTER TWO

Your Spouse is Human

> *"God grant me the courage to change the things I can change; the serenity to accept the things I cannot change, and the wisdom to know the difference."*

> *- Saint Francis Xavier*

Love is a very interesting phenomenon. It lends an "other-worldly" tinge or quality to relationships that tends to make partners see each other as saints or angels who can do no wrong. Very often this charm continues throughout courtship and by the time the haze disappears within marriage, there is disillusionment. It is with this thought in mind that we like to caution that from the beginning, partners should know that their spouses are HUMAN. As humans they are flawed. They are imperfect. They are fallible and prone to error in all its ramifications. Grace lifts us from sinner to saint but the journey to living the life of a saint is a long and onerous one. Every individual can identify with this but often do not extend that benefit to someone else, especially one's spouse.

The total package of each life is made up of the good, the bad and the ugly. A master key to a blissful marriage of which God can boast is acceptance. You must accept the total package. Rejoice in the good, tolerate the bad and the ugly and ask for grace to fulfil your God-given function of blunting the edges of the bad and ugly, and honing the good to perfection.

Maybe you have heard that love is blind but marriage is the eye-opener. This statement is true only when one takes into consideration the fact that the period of courtship is hazy no matter how long it lasts. People seem to put only their best foot forward and be on excellent behavior. It may be because they are desperate to marry the person in their lives and so they play the chameleon, but it is not always so. The fact is that in the close proximity of marriage there is a nakedness that has nothing to do with our state of undress. Sometimes we even discover aspects of ourselves we never knew existed and which leave us either shocked or pleasantly surprised. The marriage relationship can bring out the best and the worst in us. If we can learn to stand ourselves and accept that what we are seeing is the real us, then we should extend the same favor to our spouses.

We have heard it preached in many marriage seminars and other fora that women should treat their husbands as kings and lords while men should treat their wives as queens. They also add that this is part of the panacea for a blissful marriage. I agree fully with the admonition. However, the fact remains that your spouse may not want to be so treated and may not even notice your attempts at validating them.

Acceptance means that you do not ascribe to your spouse virtues that they do not possess. You may pray into their lives the things you want to see. That is different from presenting them as angels of light when indeed they are agents of darkness. Let us borrow a leaf from Abigail.

> *"Now when Abigail saw David, she dismounted quickly from the donkey, fell on her face before David, and bowed down to the ground. So, she fell at his feet and said: "On me, my lord, on me let this iniquity be! And please let your maidservant speak in your ears, and hear the words of your maidservant. Please, let not my lord regard this scoundrel Nabal. For as his name is, so is he: Nabal is his name, and folly is with him! But I, your maidservant, did not see the young men of my lord whom you sent. Now therefore, my lord, as the Lord lives and as your soul lives, since the Lord has held you back from coming to bloodshed and from avenging yourself with your own hand, now then, let your enemies and those who seek harm for my lord be as Nabal. And now this present which your maidservant has brought to my lord, let it be given to the young men who follow my lord. Please forgive the trespass of your maidservant. For the Lord will certainly make for my lord an enduring house, because my lord fights the battles of the Lord, and evil is not found in you throughout your days. Yet*

a man has risen to pursue you and seek your
life, but the life of my lord shall be bound in
the bundle of the living with the Lord your
God; and the lives of your enemies He shall
sling out, as from the pocket of a sling. And
it shall come to pass, when the Lord has done
for my lord according to all the good that He
has spoken concerning you, and has appointed
you ruler over Israel, that this will be no grief
to you, nor offense of heart to my lord, either
that you have shed blood without cause, or
that my lord has avenged himself."

- 1 Sam 25:23-31 NKJV

This is the story of how Abigail delivered her "worthless" husband from the excusable wrath of David and his men. She knew who her husband was and covered up for his weaknesses. Apparently, this was not the first time she stood in the gap. The servants knew she had good sense and was pragmatic, that was why they quickly appealed to her and she took action immediately without telling her husband.

'Now one of the young men told Abigail,
Nabal's wife, saying, "Look, David sent
messengers from the wilderness to greet our
master; and he reviled them. But the men were
very good to us, and we were not hurt, nor did
we miss anything as long as we accompanied
them, when we were in the fields. They were a
wall to us both by night and day, all the time
we were with them keeping the sheep. Now

> *therefore, know and consider what you will do, for harm is determined against our master and against all his household. For he is such a scoundrel* *that one cannot speak to him."*
>
> *Then Abigail made haste and took two hundred loaves of bread, two skins of wine, five sheep already dressed, five seahs of roasted grain, one hundred clusters of raisins, and two hundred cakes of figs, and loaded them on donkeys. And she said to her servants, "Go on before me; see, I am coming after you." But she did not tell her husband Nabal.'*

- 1 Sam 25:14-19 NKJV.

Her knowledge and ACCEPTANCE of her husband enabled her to know that appealing to him would be not only useless but counter-productive and that informed her course of action. Even though God's judgment located him soon after, Abigail's action saved members of his household who would have been victims of David's unmitigated wrath.

When we talk about acceptance in this context of marriage, we do not mean that we fold our hands, or wring them in frustration and watch impotently as the devil makes mince-meat of our spouses. I mean that we actively engage the enemy in the spiritual realm to pluck them out of satanic influences that make their bad and ugly sides an everyday affair. I mean that we contend in the place of prayer until the good is virtually all we see – until they stand perfect and complete in all God's will concerning them. I mean that we deliberately lay aside the sense of hurt we feel when the manifestation of their bad and ugly sides is directed against us – as they most often are – and rather accept to be wronged and have peace than stand on our right and lose it.

A very practical view on acceptance of one's spouse is found in a book by Dag Heward-Mills:

"It is important for every married couple to understand that people usually do not change much when they get married. Couples however can choose to be happy in their marriages when they learn to accept what they have." He goes on to list four things every married couple must accept:

i.   *Accept the temperament of your spouse.*
ii. *Accept the masculinity or femininity of your spouse.*
iii. *Accept the negative things about your spouse's character.*
iv. *Accept the physical looks and structure of your spouse.*

- (Model Marriage p.124-126).

To explain the last thing a little bit further, let us understand that we all change physically with advancing age. Just imagine if we remained physically the way we were at birth! We would not be talking marriage now. If we can accept, even celebrate the fact that we grow into adulthood, then we must also accept the fact of our decline as we progress in years. Let us also understand that the signs of decline we see in our spouse is a reflection of what is happening in our own lives. It is a measure of our love for our spouse to make the effort to keep our bodies from decline as much as possible through physical exercise, proper diet, sufficient sleep and intellectual application.

It is also important to note that to be able to accept your spouse, you must first accept yourself. You must accept your strengths as well as weaknesses.

CHAPTER THREE

Respect is Reciprocal

"*Out of respect for Christ, be courteously reverent to one another.*

Wives, understand and support your husbands in ways that show your support for Christ.

The husband provides leadership to his wife the way Christ does to his church, not by domineering but by cherishing.

So, just as the church submits to Christ as he exercises such leadership, wives should likewise submit to their husbands.

Husbands, go all out in your love for your wives, exactly as Christ did for the church — a love marked by giving, not getting.

Christ's love makes the church whole. His words evoke her beauty. Everything he does and says is designed to bring the best out of her dressing her in dazzling white silk, radiant with holiness.

And that is how husbands ought to love their wives. They're really doing themselves a favor - since they're already "one" in marriage."

- Eph 5:21-28 TMB

I have heard a husband of many years quote part of the above Scripture to excuse his lack of expression of love towards his wife. Using the King James Version which says the wife must submit to her husband as unto the Lord, he argued that this was first said before the admonition that the husband should love the wife as Christ loves the church. His argument

was that since the admonition was first to the woman, it meant the husband's love was consequent on her respect for him. In his words: "Since she does not submit to me, I can't love her". Nice argument but wrong! That is why I chose to take the Scripture in context and to use a contemporary paraphrase to aid our understanding.

It starts in verse 21 by saying that spouses should be courteous and reverent to each other, not because they deserve it, but out of reverence for Christ. That means our treatment of our spouse should be predicated on our relationship with Christ. The mutuality of this reverence is further broken down in the verses following by highlighting the woman's role and then the man's.

Wives are admonished to understand and support their husbands in a way that shows their support for Christ. Women need to take this to heart seriously. Many a marriage has fractured because of the woman's commitment to the Church. In an attempt to express their commitment to God and His work, women tend to give their time, energy and money to the church so much so that the husband feels marginalized. Not liking to play second fiddle (who does?), he kicks against the wife's church activities and is immediately labelled "carnal". Support for the cause of Christ is not only expressed through church activity. It also finds expression in the woman's attitude towards her husband's needs. God will not fault her for missing church because she chose to meet her husband's need at that time. Indeed, allowance has already been made for that in Scripture. *"...she who is married cares about the things of the world — how she may please her husband." 1 Cor. 7:34-35 NKJV.*

We are told in verse 23 that the husband provides (or should provide) leadership to his wife the way Christ does to his church, not by domineering but by cherishing. When husbands exercise such leadership, submission by the wife is not difficult. But when the woman is left to think for herself, fend for herself, dream up and execute projects by herself, what is there to submit to?

Husbands are also admonished in verses 25-28 to pull out all the stops in their bid to express love to their wives the way Christ did to the church by laying down his life. When I saw the admonition to "go all out in your love for your wives", I remembered a man who would follow his wife to the salon and choose for her the nail polish she should use. He was called all kinds of names but it did not bother him. That was one of the ways he chose to express his love and I think it was beautiful.

I have heard it said often that marriage is a give and take relationship. This is true. However, when one partner is always giving and the other always taking, how can harmony be sustained? One partner will get worn out before long. One of the peculiarities of marriage is that God designed it as a cure for human selfishness. Many arguments and disagreements start with statements like; "Who does he take me for?" "Does he think I am a fool?" "When I finish with him, he will know that he tangoed with the wrong bae." This shows us that where self is given unfettered expression, marriage cannot be successful.

> *Therefore, if there is any consolation in Christ, if any comfort of love, if any fellowship of the Spirit, if any affection and mercy, fulfill my joy by being like-minded, having the same love, being of one accord, of one mind. Let nothing be done through selfish ambition or conceit, but in lowliness of mind let each esteem others better than himself. Let each of you look out not only for his own interests, but also for the interests of others.*
>
> *- Phil 2:1-4 NKJV*

This Scripture though addressed to the church universal, can arguably find its best expression and most useful purpose within the context of marriage. This is so because in marriage interests are so intertwined and often contrasting as to sometimes be annoying. Only by deliberately putting your partner first can you produce, sustain and enhance harmony. This is as true in the choice of what to eat, when and where, to how many children to have, what church to attend and when, where and how to have sex.

Even though there is the element of spontaneity in the

activities of marriage, there is an undergirding element of thought, discussion, choice and planning without which one of the parties might find themselves at the receiving end of exploitation. That is why the letter "I" must be whittled down to the barest minimum for a marriage to be blissful. Let me quickly mention that this whittling down of the "I" does not diminish either of the spouses, rather it validates them. The Message Bible continues by saying that the love of Christ for the church is characterized by giving and not by taking. It makes the church whole, evokes her beauty and majors in words and acts designed to bring the best out of her. Obviously, this is a tall order for the human male who looks for the most beautiful, intelligent, sexy, and connected female to marry in order to show off his acquisition or get the right connections. Few are the men who marry in order to improve the woman. No matter what your reasons were for choosing your wife, when you have married her, you as a husband must strive to ensure that she improves. Let her blossom in your hands not only with a pot-belly but with a greater knowledge of God, greater academic attainment, better clothes, more poise, name it. And because you cannot give what you don't have, you must go that way first.

Some men married women who were more academically advanced than they. It is a disservice to your wife for you to remain in that state after marriage. You should seek to improve yourself. However, your attitude and reasons are important. Do it because you know it will make her happy. Discuss it with her and solicit her help. You are in this together. Respect her opinion. Let her help you make your choices. Make full use of that nebulous phenomenon called feminine intuition which Edwin Biayeibo has called "gift of suspicion". (Women, Save our Men p.55).

And the wife also that married a man not as highly educated or connected as you, must learn to respect him as your head. No-one put a gun to your head to say you must marry him. No matter what informed your choice, you chose him. Having made that choice, you must respect it and respect him. You may not always agree with him but learn to show him in loving and subtle ways that even when you disagree with him it is for his own good and the good of your relationship. Understand that there are many ways of approaching a problem and agree to try his way sometimes even if it is not the best way. And if the outcome is less than what was desired, try not to say "I told you so". Do not flaunt your "supremacy". You will sometimes, maybe often, have to accept positions less than what your potential allows. You may have to accept a social status below what you feel is rightfully yours. You may be a star in obscurity for a very long time. You might feel like throwing in the towel again and again. And pray, lady, pray.

CHAPTER FOUR

Together Without Smothering

"Submitting to one another in the fear of God"

- Eph. 5:21 NKJV

Many people looking at marriage from outside fear to go in because they feel they will lose their identity. That is why someone thought up the sick joke that the smallest pair of handcuffs ever manufactured is the wedding rings. I think this sense of loss is worse for the female than the male but I may be wrong. Why I think it is worse for the female is that she is the one who loses her name which is the first mark of identity. She loses her origins and pedigree, and especially in inter-tribal or inter-cultural marriages, she has to learn and imbibe an alien culture and make it her own. I remember a friend of mine who applied for work in one of the government ministries. The family happened to be living in her state of origin whereas she had been married out. As a result of marriage her new name had nothing to show where she was from. It was when she submitted her credentials that still bore her maiden name that the interviewers knew she was from their place and that weighed favorably for her. She could easily have lost a good job opportunity because of marriage.

The male also has that sense of suffocation. He cannot hang out with the boys like he used to do. Some ribald jokes that were his stock-in-trade have to be tempered if he does not want his wife to be at the receiving end of some of them. I have heard a young husband quarrelling with his bride and saying: "because of you I have lost all my friends". Some who come from large families who loved doing things together suddenly find themselves at a loose end when they have only this one person for company day in, day out. The situation becomes more complicated if his spouse came from a self-sufficient background and was probably an only child.

Let us establish first of all that affiliations will be radically altered by marriage. The first quarrel I had with my in-laws had to do with these changing affiliations. They had a tradition in which food was cooked and served together. It was a beautiful tradition which I did not understand because where I came from food was served us in different plates though we almost always ate together. Eating from the same plate was an alien practice to me. When I got married, I found that my husband could not eat alone so I would put my food and his in the same plate and we would eat together. We still do after almost forty years and I love it – most of the time. Oh, where are those smileys? What I failed to understand was that I was expected to serve food in a big platter or tray so that we and his siblings could eat together anytime we all happened to be home at the same time. What they failed to understand was that things had changed and he was now putting hands together with me in the plate, and not with them. It resulted in a major dispute but I thank God for a quiet, peace-loving father-in-law who was able to douse the flames and restore peace in record time and help me ease gradually into the changes that came with marriage.

A sense of smothering comes when a spouse expects the other to adjust automatically to the new life imposed on them by marriage. To contain this, it is necessary to constantly remind ourselves that our spouse had a life before marriage that is not terminated automatically when one gets married and that they probably enjoyed that life more than the one they are entering into. Even if they did not enjoy it more, it was more familiar terrain. We must therefore act with understanding, use loving words, do not be unnecessarily critical. Let your criticisms be more constructive than scathing.

Women have a tendency to cry with little provocation. A wise husband will study to know how best to interact with her at such times. "Don't cry" may evoke more tears. Ignoring her may trigger the next world war. Saying things like; "what nonsense is this?" will make you out to be a cad of the highest order. I heard of one who left the house for hours and the first thing he said on his return was; "have you finished crying?"

Though I cannot give you an answer that will work 100% of the time, my advice is: Give her space. If you can stand the tears stay close by and give her a back or leg rub, or hand her a much-needed handkerchief. If you cannot, then go out and return before too long. Don't return empty-handed. Buy her something – flowers, candy and peppered-fish. Not handkerchiefs please.

There are situations where silence is golden. Some people cannot be silent for any length of time. They think every moment has to be filled with words. Most times it is the women that do most of those not-well-thought-out talking. It can be really irritating. Society somehow accepts, even expects this from women just as it expects a man to indulge in extra-marital affairs. When it is the man that does the non-stop talking, it can really be off-putting. Learn the art of companionable silence. Women must learn when talk is superfluous. We women sometimes talk so much, giving minute and unnecessary details that a man would wonder what he is getting himself into by asking the simple question; "how was your day?"

Some people come into marriage with hammers, nails and lashing to tinker with the personality, attitudes and character of the spouse to make them conform to their ways. That is error. The conformity will come spontaneously as you continue lovingly preferring the other above self. That is why as spouses age together, they tend to look more like each other. When you try to force conformity, you will enforce crisis. Togetherness in marriage must be the kind that brings out the best in each of the parties and if that can be achieved by not begrudging him the occasional football game with his buddies, or her, the shopping spree with the girls, then by all means, let go. When we have consideration for each other, we will set ourselves boundaries which we will not cross. And we will trust our spouse to do same.

Another area of potential conflict is that of finance. Largely gone are the days when men went out to work and the women kept home and all their financial needs were met by their men. In today's world, women are working at high profile jobs. Some are highly successful entrepreneurs and men are falling over themselves to marry such women. It is saddening that after marriage, some men would insist that the wife must not work but stay at home and take care of the family. Sometimes they are not even capable of meeting the needs of the wife, let alone that of the children. One pastor's wife was so frustrated when she found she was pregnant with their sixth child, with little coming from the husband who strictly forbade her from getting a job, engaging in a trade or even offering lessons at home. And she was a qualified teacher with mathematics as her major. "Hot cake", I would say. She was suffering in silence and contemplating an abortion. With a little counselling and some financial support, she was able to overcome the challenge. The husband was led to renew his mind and things started looking up for them. In today's Nigerian context, very few can afford life's necessities with only one source of income. There is no need to stifle the woman's money-making potential. The woman should understand as well that her husband is still head of the home notwithstanding how much she earns. They should work out a plan under God of how to handle their finances. Some churches have rules and regulations about how spouses should handle their finances. Some make operating joint accounts compulsory. While not encouraging people to run afoul of the church's instructions, it is good for the two people involved to agree on how they will handle their finances even before they marry. Especially where there are extended family ties and relationship issues, this is a matter that cannot be ignored or left until issues arise. The fear that when a woman works and earns her salary, she might no longer respect the husband is a very present and well validated one. However, under God and godly mentors this can be dealt with. When a man is self-assured, he will be able to handle himself well even if the wife earns higher, is better known or is more successful. It is not a matter of you and her, but us.

Under God, the wife's shine does not reduce that of the husband, rather it increases it. Consider this reference to the Proverb 31 woman;

"Her husband is known in the gates, When he sits among the elders of the land". Prov. 31:23 NKJV. Does this sound like one who is eclipsed by his wife's profile? No. Rather he is enhanced and validated by it.

CHAPTER FIVE

Communication is Key

*"Be angry, and do not sin" do not let the
sun go down on your wrath, nor give place to
the devil." Eph. 4:26,27 NKJV*

In every human relationship, communication is
important. However, in marriage, maybe more than in any
other relationship, the place of effective communication
cannot be overemphasized. Indeed, without communication
there can be no real relationship. This is so because in
marriage the spouses virtually live in each other's *'pocket'*
and it can get intensely "hot" if either is misunderstood. Let
me re-emphasize that we are looking at the ideal marriage –
the Christian marriage being lived out in a non-Christian
world. In such a marriage, divorce is not an option.
Separation neither. Effective communication is therefore
an absolute necessity if the partners must find satisfaction
in their marriage.

What then is communication? For our context, we
would take the definition that says: "The concept or state

of exchanging data or information between two entities". The entities here are husband and wife. It is only when you communicate that you can talk about your problems, share your dreams, hopes and fears and by so doing deepen the bond you share as lovers. As you open up to each other there is better accommodation and understanding. That is a vital part of being "naked and unashamed".

It has been said that opposites attract and that is true. How else would spouses complement each other? The differences in the spouses over and above that of gender is what makes the relationship spicey. It is also what rounds out the perspectives and makes you exclaim again and again in awesome wonder: "wow, I never saw it that way" when your spouse gives his/her take on a matter. Early in the relationship, these differences are easy to accept and appreciate but as time goes on, the rut sets in and we tend to see the very differences we admired as faults, hindrances and even blights. This is precisely why communication needs to be learned and worked on. It does not come spontaneously.

Communication involves both giving and receiving. You receive when you listen and you give when you… I was going to say speak…but I had to pause because there is more to it than just speaking. Giving involves the expression of thoughts and feelings. These four elements are identifiable: Verbal messages (What is said), contextual issues (how it is said), emotional tone (why it is said) and non-verbal cues (what is left unsaid).

Listening is a skill or an art that needs to be learnt and cultivated. This is so because we all love to be heard. We even like to hear the sound of our own voice and depending on our temperament, how we were brought up and our exposure, we like to speak and listening does not come naturally. Listening also requires a certain level of sensitivity. You may be married to a partner who came from a background of bullying, whether covert or overt. They may have gotten used to being put down, their opinions being discounted. If they come into marriage with this baggage, it will take a sensitive, listening partner to draw them out and help them value their opinions sufficiently to express them. Effective listening involves concentration, understanding and empathy. Concentration means you give undivided attention to your spouse when he/or she is giving information or data. That might be the time to pause the football game or the movie, put a page marker in the book or exit the game or other app on your phone. It is actually rude to be pressing your phone when your spouse is trying to speak with you. Also, sensitivity is required for the one trying to speak to request the other to please give me this time. Understanding means you don't just listen; you actively involve your intellect in the subject of discussion. You receive the information, process it and have a view waiting for expression at the right time. Empathy means you put yourself in your spouse's shoes and try to see the object of his discussion from his perspective.

When speaking, it is important to be careful not only of what you say but also how you say it. It is said that action and reaction are equal and opposite. This plays out graphically in the use of words, the attitude with which the words are used, and the perceived body language of the speaker. That is why the Bible gives the injunction to speak the truth in love (Ephesians 4:15). These three words: Speaking, Truth, In-love are important elements in effective communication.

Speaking

It is important to speak and communicate frequently and clearly to your spouse about what is really going inside of you. Your spouse is not a mind reader and expecting him/her to know what you feel inside is unacceptable. One should not be afraid to be transparent and vulnerable.

The Truth

We often do speak but don't speak the truth. Especially in conflict situations when we are trying to win an argument or prove a point. Each spouse should endeavor to speak the truth and avoid exaggeration. When there is conflict, couples should also avoid casting aspersions on each other's character. The focus should be on the issues of conflict. It is important to pay attention to the body language of your spouse for cues on how to respond appropriately.

In Love

It is possible to speak the absolute truth but to do it in a way that is cutting and hurtful. "Your breath stinks" may be a 100% true statement but will not help your relationship. The scriptures teaches us to speak the truth, but to do it in love – Ephesians 4:15. Colossians

4:6 also encourages to let our conversations always be full of grace and seasoned with salt.

Temperamental considerations should not be ignored. Effective communication is not easy. It is a learning process and requires a large dose of patience and constant practice. It does not guarantee that you will not have any more problems as a couple but it means you stand a good chance of solving them in record time, and understanding the meaning of "cleaving" while you are at it.

We will conclude this communication discourse by looking at some hindrances to effective communication in the hope that as we identify the problem, we will do the necessary to find and effect a solution.

The emotional and physical state of the parties can be a hindrance. Hunger, anxiety, anger, sadness and exhaustion are some of the factors that can affect one's ability to listen and interact effectively. If your spouse is just returning from a stressful day at work, that is scarcely the best time to raise the matter of children's school fees or the house rent. If one of the spouses stammers, this can also pose a barrier which with loving understanding and patience from both sides, can even result in an interesting twist to conversations which other people would not experience.

Style of communication can be a barrier. This is very common in inter-tribal or cross-cultural marriages. Some tribes tend to talk loudly and sometimes when you hear their normal discussions you might think they are quarrelling. If one of the spouses came from a background where the opposite is the case, there is the tendency to think she is shouting when all she is doing is "being herself". Visiting with her siblings and watching them interact might help you understand her better.

What of interruptions? Children crying, bringing work home, social media and television are some of the major culprits. Sometimes even Bible reading and prayer can be interruptions. Let us learn to give our spouses their time, and God his own. There is time for everything is an important fact to remember here.

Nagging wears out both the giver and the taker. Spouses should learn to say what they have to say and leave it at that.

There is a lot more that can be said about hindrances to good communication between spouses. However, what is important is the willingness to do the needful. It is true that where there is a will, there is a way. Be proactive about removing the hindrances. Your marriage is meant to be enjoyed, not endured.

CHAPTER SIX

Family Matters

> *"But Ruth said;' Entreat me not to leave you; or to turn back from following you; For wherever you go, I will go; And wherever you lodge, I will lodge; Your people shall be my people, and your God, my God..."'Ruth 1:16 NKJV*

Marriage comes with the introduction of new affiliations and ties. Without marriage there would be no in-laws (Father-in-law, mother-in-law etc.) Where there has been the death of a spouse, or a child out of wedlock, or divorce and remarriage, there is also the step-relationship. These new affiliations take their toll on the marriage, sometimes threatening its very existence. All relationships need to be put in proper perspective if the marriage must speak well of Christ and the church.

> *"The couple who wishes to build a strong marriage should, in their early married*

*life, invest time and effort in cementing
the marriage bond, while redefining their
connection to their original families. While
old loyalties to both sets of parents continue in
the lives of the couple, they ought to redefine
these, so that their new loyalties to each other
comes first." (Dag Heward-Mills 113).*

The new loyalty is to your immediate spouse. As we consider family matters therefore, we will first differentiate between the nuclear and the extended family. The nuclear family is made up of the husband, the wife and the children. The children may be biological or adopted. Every marriage has its own challenges. In fact, marriage itself is a very challenging institution. I remain constantly amazed at how two people from different families, backgrounds, cultures, sometimes religions happen to meet at a point in time and that meeting translates into marriage. What happened to all the meetings with others more compatible and having more commonalities? No wonder the apostle Paul says it is a mystery!

No matter how close the bond between a child and his parents is, the bond between a husband and wife is closer. More often than not, tensions arise between the mothers of husbands and their son's wife than between any other in-law relationship as mothers tend to have a great difficulty giving up their sons. That is usually because of the ill-conceived notion that the new bride is coming to displace her in the son's affections. Such mothers put roadblocks in the paths of a new wife, conveniently forgetting that they themselves were new brides at some time in their lives. Others want to pay back to their son's wife the misery they endured at the hands of their mother-in-law. These are warped ways of thinking. From the beginning the husband must let it be known that he and his wife are an entity. Especially where there is disparity in social status between the husband's family and the wife's, the husband must show a lot of sensitivity and shield the wife from ridicule while schooling her on expected etiquette. The wife also needs to be willing to adapt. She now belongs to a family different from the one she grew up in. This marriage car has no reverse gear so the sooner she adapts the better. She will need to make friends with her husband's siblings without being unduly ingratiating or self-effacing. In all these changing scenarios, it is important to limit discussing your spouse with your parents or siblings. A lady was in the habit of running to her mother every time she had a misunderstanding with the husband. She would tell her in lurid details the cause of the quarrel and what the man had said and done. However, when they sorted out their issues and life went back to normal, she never remembered to fill the mother in. The mother therefore grew to have a very jaundiced view of the son-in-law and wondered what her daughter was still doing in a marriage that caused her so much pain. She refused to visit the family despite repeated invitations-she did not want to witness the monster maltreat her daughter. However, she had no choice but to go and stay with them as a result of a health challenge. She was surprised to see her daughter interacting lovingly and playfully with her husband and the husband responding in kind. It was when she commented on it that the daughter realized how she had sold a bad image of her husband to her mother. It was then she also realized that all her tattle tales to her mother did not add value to her marriage.

Having said this, we must remark that we are not advocating exclusivity and ostracism. In Africa we still enjoy the sweetness of extended family relationships. A popular song in Efik says in part: "Okuk ikpo-ikpu ofong ikpu-ikpu; owo edi inyene". Meaning that money and clothes are valueless; true wealth is people. It is therefore important to cultivate healthy interpersonal relationships in these new equations. Ruth was able to do this with Naomi and, see where it landed her!

> *But Ruth said: "Entreat me not to leave you, Or to turn back from following after you;*
> *For wherever you go, I will go; And wherever you lodge, I will lodge;*
> *Your people shall be my people, And your God, my God.*
> *Where you die, I will die, And there will I be buried.*
> *The Lord do so to me, and more also, If anything but death parts you and me."*
> *When she saw that she was determined to go with her, she stopped speaking to her"*
>
> *- Ruth 1:16-18 NKJV*

> *So, Boaz took Ruth and she became his wife; and when he went in to her, the Lord gave her conception, and she bore a son. Then the women said to Naomi, "Blessed be the Lord, who has not left you this day without*

> *a close relative; and may his name be famous*
> *in Israel! And may he be to you a restorer of*
> *life and a nourisher of your old age; for your*
> *daughter-in-law, who loves you, who is better*
> *to you than seven sons, has borne him."*

- Ruth 4:13-16 NKJV

You may not always agree with your mother-in-law, but try not to disrespect her. Do your best not to push your husband to the point where he has to make a choice between you and his mother. There is enough good in you to overcome whatever evil your motherinlaw may throw your way. Do not join the band of women who pray for the death of their mother-in-law even before they enter the marriage. Remember that by the grace of God you too will be a mother-in-law someday.

There is no difficulty that a husband and wife cannot solve together at the foot of the cross. To do this there has to be openness. *And they were both naked, the man and his wife, and were not ashamed.* Gen. 2:25 NKJV. The husband and wife should be open and honest with each other even before marriage. There should be no cause for suspicion. This is so because it is often in the bid to unravel some mystery arising from the secretiveness of a spouse that the other goes out to ask questions and tell tales in the process. Where there is transparency, the need for tales is taken away.

An imperative that will enhance leaving and cleaving of a new couple is their living arrangements. *Therefore, shall a man leave his father and his mother, and shall cleave unto his wife: and they shall be one flesh.* Gen 2:24 (KJV). I have always been baffled by the fact that though the Bible says a man shall leave father and mother, it is usually the woman that leaves. However, I am sure God knew what he was saying when he said the man should leave. The woman will leave anyway – leave her home, leave her name, leave her friends – just LEAVE.

The first step is to leave physically. Marrying your new bride and bringing her to the family house, especially in this dispensation, is courting disaster. Please get a place of your own no matter how small. Come and visit the homestead for short intervals and go back. Let the woman adjust to living with you first before having to adjust to the vagaries of all other of your family members especially your mother. When your parents and/or siblings come to visit, welcome them and try not to show a preference for them over your wife. Show by words and action that your wife is in control of your home. Of course, you will be called names like "woman wrapper" or worse. Never take sides with your family against your wife. Even when she is wrong, support and defend her in public. When you are alone together you can lovingly show her where she was wrong. This advice goes both ways.

The next step is to leave emotionally. Your wife is not your mother so stop comparing them. Her cooking is going to be different from your mother's. Learn to love her cooking because she's going to be doing it for you for a long time, and believe me, she will get better especially if you encourage her. Also, your taste buds will adjust to her level of salt, pepper and seasoning. Appreciate her efforts at pleasing you. Find out how she likes to be appreciated. Every woman loves to hear: "Darling, your food is delicious". Saying "thank you" does not cover it.

To the wife also, your husband is not your father. A story is told of a beloved Christian couple at the verge of divorce. The wife thought the husband very uncaring because he never made time to help her with the laundry. She was raised by a single father because her mum died when she was a baby and the father refused to remarry because he did not want anyone maltreating his children. Even after she left home and started work, the father would visit and do her accumulated laundry for her and sometimes even do her shopping and cooking. She entered into marriage with the notion that this was the hallmark of a caring man. That her husband not only did not do these for her but expected her to do them for him showed he did not care. The husband did not help matters. He not only failed to get her the help she so needed, but used every opportunity to point out what he saw as her deficiencies as a wife. Thank God for timely intervention, this issue and others were resolved and the marriage was saved. Truly, everyone carries baggage. That is why we need each other.

Another area of conflict within the family is with the husband's siblings. The sisters of the husband usually look at the new wife as an interloper. They use every opportunity they find to harass, intimidate and malign the poor girl. Unfortunately, they can do it in such an innocuous manner that their brother might not even notice. The wife may not say anything because she does not want to be accused of driving a wedge between her husband and his siblings. This calls for sensitivity on the part of the husband. He must learn to listen in two dimensions and hear what is said from what is not said. He must hear, not only what is being said, but the way it is being said especially if the sisters had female friends that often visited. It is possible they had hopes of their brother marrying one of their friends and that could lead to them resenting the woman he finally married.

Keeping it within the family implies that the only third party allowed in your marriage is the Holy Spirit. Learn to pray together, fast together, study Scriptures together, work out together, bath together, have sex together, wash plates together, cook together, browse together, laugh together and cry together. The list is actually inexhaustible so you can add your own. Where there is a problem in any of these *'togethernesses'*, then discuss with the Holy Spirit and He will show you how to go about correcting it.

I learnt this lesson in a hard but effective way early in my marriage. I was trying to get my husband to take a decision on a matter of crucial importance. I don't have a problem taking split-second decisions and accepting responsibility for the outcome. My husband on the other hand takes a long time to reach his decisions but scarcely ever has reason to regret the decision once taken. I had not learnt that yet, so I kept at him to take the decision. It caused an unnecessary strain on our relationship more so because, though I was asking him to take a stand, I was actually expecting him to endorse the stand I had taken. One day as I was praying and worrying over the issue, I heard the Spirit whisper in my spirit "You are speaking to the wrong person". There and then I decided to follow my husband on the matter and never mentioned the issue again. Wonder of wonders, the very next day he took a stand, and it was what I wanted all the while! Don't nag, don't fret. Talk to the Holy Spirit and patiently wait. Your response may not be as automatic as mine but it will certainly come, and will be as astounding. Remember a part of the song "What A friend We Have in Jesus" which says:

"Oh, what peace we often forfeit, oh
what needless pain we bear
All because we do not carry, Everything to God in prayer"

CHAPTER SEVEN

Having Sex Versus Making Love

"Relish life with the spouse you love each
and every day of your precarious life.
Each day is God's gift. It's all you get in
exchange for the hard work of staying alive.
Make the most of each one!"

- Eccl 9:9 TMB

There are varying opinions about what Tim LaHaye calls The Marriage Act but I will call plainly Sex. The issue of sex is intriguing even from a very tender age. There is a curiosity about the private parts of the body which may inadvertently be caused by parents who either by plain words or undue caution pass on the information that these parts are indeed private – no go areas. It all started in the Garden of Eden when the eating of the forbidden fruit gave rise to sexual awareness:

"So, when the woman saw that the tree was good for food, that it was pleasant to the eyes, and a tree desirable to make one wise, she took of its fruit and ate. She also gave to her husband with her, and he ate. Then the eyes of both of them were opened, and they knew that they were naked; and they sewed fig leaves together and made themselves coverings."

- Gen 3:6-7 NKJV

And so, in line with the biblical thought that stolen waters are sweet, some start experimenting with sex early in life possibly to their detriment when they do get married.

Let us state clearly here that God knowingly placed sex within the ambits of marriage. In His plan, there is no sex outside marriage. We may not know whether He created Adam as a child and allowed him to grow to maturity before introducing him to Eve. What is clear is that Eve was a fully grown woman who was given to him as a wife.

'And the Lord God caused a deep sleep to fall on Adam, and he slept; and He took one of his ribs, and closed up the flesh in its place. Then the rib which the Lord God had taken from man He made into a woman, and He brought her to the man.

And Adam said: "This is now bone of my bones and flesh of my flesh;

She shall be called Woman, because she was taken out of Man."

*Therefore, a man shall leave his father
and mother and be joined to his wife, and
they shall become one flesh.'*

- Gen 2:21-24.

It is reasonable to believe that the joining here is referring – at least in part – to sexual intercourse. That is why many believe that having sex is doing what comes naturally. That is also why I like to differentiate between having sex and making love and to state that while having sex may be doing what comes naturally, making love is a very different ball game. While having sex is the natural culmination of the physical attraction between a man and a woman, making love is a covenant act of mutual giving and taking between a man and his wife that brings satisfaction to both. I believe that what God had in mind was for the husband and wife to make love while having sex, and we will spend some time to explore the pros and cons of this wonderful experience.

There are so many misconceptions, taboos and injunctions concerning sexual love that many approach marriage and lovemaking with fear. Others, in a bid to show their independence throw caution to the winds and dabble into experimentation which often leaves a bad taste in the mouth (metaphorically speaking) or unpalatable experiences that end with "had I known". Some of these taboos differ with differing race, culture and religion. No matter your view of sexual love or your experiences before now, it is good to know that God does not leave us alone on this journey. This is one of the areas in which, if well handled, I see

God nodding with satisfaction and declaring like He did at creation; "Very Good".

This sounds like an idyll which many desire, even strive for but never reach. Some even wonder whether it is possible. However, we can rest assured that it is possible. It is what God had in mind when He made us male and female and as we align with Him, we will get there. Unfortunately, many godly people still have the notion at the back of their minds that sex is somehow ungodly or unspiritual or even dirty. That is why some couples will pray together every night except on the nights they are going to make love. They compartmentalize their lives into spiritual and unspiritual activity and sexual intercourse falls squarely into the latter category. God is involved in every aspect of our lives including our sexual journey. He is present – always and everywhere – also in the physical union.

No wonder the all-wise and all-loving God designed marriage to last a lifetime. This idyll may take a lifetime for some to discover, but certainly a lifetime may not even be enough to enjoy its benefits. It is this journey of discovery that will engage the rest of this chapter and the next.

In order to enjoy a healthy and vibrant sex life, it is necessary to understand and enjoy the fact that men and women are different and this difference goes way beyond the physical. In terms of attitude towards sex, the difference is clear. For the man mostly, sex is an act, whereas for the woman it is a life. The experience of men occurs quickly and suddenly like fire and then dies down quickly too. For women, the experience is slower and needs to be fanned. Once ablaze, the fire lasts longer.

Many women are not aware of how much capacity they

have for giving and accepting sexual pleasure because they have never had the chance of expressing themselves. Their husbands start and finish before their wives even start. They think that sex is something a man does to a woman, not realizing that it is something a man and a woman do TOGETHER. That is why women commonly complain that men love sex too much and men complain that women are stingy in their response to sex. The fact is that a woman loves and needs sex as much as a man but their approaches are different. A man can compartmentalize sex, push aside disagreements and quarrels and finish the act without any qualms. If it is less satisfying than sometimes, he just feels it goes with the terrain – you win some and lose some. For the woman, everything is in one package. You cannot quarrel with her, ignore her the whole day, be insensitive to her needs, not listen to how her day was, and when you get into bed you want to have sex and you expect her to want it too. No. She feels used, she feels exploited, and her self-esteem plummets. If she accepts to have sexual intercourse under these circumstances, she does it as a duty. No wonder someone has said that there are no frigid women, only clumsy men. So basically, having sex is doing what comes naturally but making love is learning together how to give and take sexual pleasure for the maximum satisfaction that God intended when He created us male and female and pronounced that it was very good.

Learning together under God involves taking sex out of the gutter where Satan has put it and putting it on the lofty pedestal where it belongs. That is why I have a problem with couples watching pornography in an attempt to learn how to please each other. There is more pleasure in allowing your imagination to run riot and seeing where that takes you than in trying to do what someone else did in the hope of getting a similar result. And sex is supposed to be sacred and secret to the partners involved. Pornography cheapens it. For Christian couples to watch pornography to learn satisfactory sex is a device of the enemy to cheapen it. You can be sure that the couples producing those pornographic movies are not married. If you have been caught in this web please repent. Don't put that pressure on your spouse! Or on yourself.

CHAPTER EIGHT

A More Excellent Way

> *And yet I show you a more excellent way. 1 Cor. 12:31.*
>
> *Love suffers long and is kind; love does not envy; love does not parade itself, is not puffed up; does not behave rudely, does not seek its own, is not provoked, thinks no evil: does not rejoice in iniquity, but rejoices in the truth; bears all things, believes all things, hopes all things, endures all things. Love never fails. 1 Cor. 13:4-8.*

We will try in this chapter to be more specific about the dynamics of the sexual union. In the previous chapter we have established the fact that the woman's approach to sex is different, maybe opposite to a man's own. One is left to wonder then what God had in mind bringing these opposite approaches together in this inevitable dance of love. Was it just to satisfy His curious sense of humor or did He have a higher purpose? I am inclined to think it is the latter. God is too good and caring to try to derive humor at the expense of human discomfort. However, He is selfless and giving and desires to raise offspring of His own ilk. It is in this place of shared sexual bliss, perhaps more than in anyplace else, that the man and woman are expected to derive optimal satisfaction by suspending or downplaying their own satisfaction, concentrate on giving the partner satisfaction and end up in the aha moment they have been striving for through eons of selfish taking.

You have a lifetime to learn together the parts of your body and how they affect your libido. Find out each other's erogenous zones and how, where and when they function. This is so because, especially for the woman, there is something you do in the kitchen or bathroom and she gets wet downstairs but the same action in the bedroom at night puts her off and dries her out. Men are attracted by what they see, so sexy panties, leopard skin tights, sheer lingerie – or nothing at all – may be guaranteed to put a man in the mood in a split second. However, a woman is attracted by loving words, a soft touch, good personal hygiene, remembered birthdays and anniversaries, and a present for just-nothing at all. When your wife enters the bathroom at bedtime, invite yourself even if she does not invite you. The very act of taking that bath at that time may be screaming: "I need you" and if you respond negatively you might be rejecting her without knowing. Don't be surprised if, when you turn to her as she gets into bed, she is unresponsive.

It is important for the woman to be conversant with the female anatomy. The woman must learn to love her body and discover how to use it well for the pleasure of both herself and her husband. She must brutally expunge from her psyche the notion that sexual enjoyment for the woman is sinful and her responsibility is to "give it to him" as a duty. When her body "talks to her" she should welcome it with relish and pull out all stops to make sure she gets her husband to respond accordingly. This is exciting for the husband. Blessed indeed is that husband whose wife heeds these instructions. She must not allow the fear of an unwanted pregnancy rob her of the pleasure that is a gift of God. The same God has graciously given knowledge on methods of contraception. A visit to your health provider should help you make the choices suitable for you. Let us be quick to say here that decision on contraceptive methods should not be left to the wife. The husband and wife are in it together.

She should also be conversant with the male anatomy and gradually but surely lose that virginal shyness or even antipathy that makes her say "yuk" at the sight of a naked male. This is not just any male – he is your male. Begin to experiment by touching him. Start with the parts you admire – those bulging biceps, the strange facial and chest hairs (where applicable), the square jaw, nose, springy hair. From there you can explore the "*strange*" areas – the belly button, the hard buttocks – so different from your own – that strange appendage called the penis which can look flaccid, harmless, even pathetic at one moment and the next? Oh my! The husband needs to patiently allow these explorations and relax into, and enjoy it. She needs to find out that touching the shaft of the penis produces a different sensation and result than rubbing the tip. And that though his breasts may not be as prominent as hers, and do not produce milk normally, they are just as sensational.

The husband also needs to love his body first. He should see it as God's gift to him, not just for his personal satisfaction, but for the satisfaction of his wife. He must inform and educate his body to fulfil that mandate. Also, he must study the female anatomy which, without a doubt is more complicated than his own. He needs to know that there are other parts of a woman's body than lips, breast and vagina and that a soft breath behind her neck can make her beg for that kiss he is dying to get. He must find the clitoris and know how to manipulate that little knob for optimal results both for him and for her. Books on giving sexual pleasure to a woman are mostly written by men as most women are too reticent about discussing what makes them tick. A man might get disturbed and frustrated when, after rubbing the wife's clitoris and wet-fingering it for a good length of time he still does not get the explosion he was promised in the literature. You need to know that quite often, what the woman wants initially is not rubbing or wet-fingering. What she might want is for you to just leave your finger there and feel the pulse. While everything in you screams "rub", just hold that finger there until she jerks. This might be the signal for him to give rein to his desire for exploration.

Side by side with knowing your anatomy and that of your spouse is the willingness to explore, experiment and innovate. Young couples will find it easier to experiment for several reasons: they are young, strong and flexible and for them sex is still much of a novelty. I advise that you do not waste this time. Explore different sex positions. Explore different sex locations. Be as brazen as decency allows. You are young only once. For older couples, don't let the spark die.

Find ways to spice it up within affordable limits. Obviously sexual excitement is experienced and expressed differently with age. The following analysis may be instructive.

Sex in the 30's

When in their 30's women gain more sexual confidence and begin to take initiative during lovemaking. Many are not passive as they were when younger. Women in their 30's are more expressive about their sexual needs and their need for orgasm… Some men may find this sudden change in their previously compliant wives rather frightening (while) others will welcome her initiative and respond positively. The men too are now more concerned about what brings satisfaction to their partners…

Sex in the 40's

Usually, as women approach the end of their childbearing years at age forty, they often find more opportunity to focus on themselves, and therefore blossom. This is reflected in a more fulfilling sex life. Both men and women in their forties have attained some measure of emotional maturity and have overcome sexual *inadequacies*. Each appreciates what the other likes and sex is better…

Sex in the 50's

A lot of men are anxious about their sexual life when approaching their 50's, fearing that sex will not be as exciting as it was in their youth. While it is true that erections are usually less frequent, the advantage is that the erections that older men do get will last longer and they will find sex more satisfying. Since the compulsion to ejaculate is significantly reduced, there is abundant time for foreplay, and the expression of warmth and intimacy by partners. Women need to learn though that their fifty-something-year-old husband may now be satisfied without ejaculating, and may no longer be aroused merely by sight... *The men must also understand that failure to ejaculate does not reduce them in any way and not overburden the wife seeking an ejaculation that refuses to come.* (Italics mine).

Sex in the 60's

Interestingly, couples in their sixties and after may actually find their sexual experience most gratifying, even though sex is infrequent. Women in this age group have recurrent orgasms, and the men when strong physically can be quite virile. (Model Marriage-Dag Heward-Mills pp262-264)

Whatever age bracket you belong to, choose to enjoy your life with your mate. Be unselfish. This is one area of life where you receive more personal satisfaction as you give. Your target should be to arrive at orgasm together. If you do not get it right the first, second or tenth time around, don't worry. Keep working at it, after all you have a whole lifetime.

CHAPTER NINE

The Icing

Behold, children are a heritage from the Lord, The fruit of the womb is a reward.

Like arrows in the hand of a warrior, So are the children of one's youth.

Happy is the man who has his quiver full of them;

They shall not be ashamed, But shall speak with their enemies in the gate.

- Ps 127:3-5 NKJV.

Metaphors are a poignant and interesting way to drive home a point. Jesus used a lot of metaphors in his teaching ministry as he spoke in parables. In the same way, I would like to use the metaphor of a cake to describe the next aspect of marriage. The confection industry has waxed strong and innovative in recent times and the making of wedding cakes, birthday cakes, anniversary cakes and others has become a very lucrative business.

Cakes come in all kinds of flavors: chocolate, vanilla, cinnamon, you name it. Cakes can be made in tiers and we can have father cake, mother cake, children cake and cousin cake. The greater the imagination of the baker, the more unique the cake will be. As a matter of fact, one of the things people look forward to seeing and commenting on at a wedding is the cake. However, what makes the cake attractive is not the flavor but the icing. The icing brings color and really showcases the art of the confectioner.

At the time of this writing, the Women's Missionary Union of the Nigerian Baptist Convention has just celebrated her centenary. One of the unforgettable features of that celebration was the variety of cakes baked by various units of the Union. There were cakes by individuals, churches, Associations, Conferences and of course the mother of all - the Convention. Even though there was no competition, each new cake seemed to outdo the last one. It was beautiful.

By now you may be wondering what all this cake story has to do with marriage so let me satisfy your curiosity. We are using the cake as a metaphor for marriage. Here the cake itself is the marriage- the husband and his wife- and the icing is the children. The icing beautifies the cake and makes it attractive by introducing or adding color. People "uh" and "ah" over the cake because of the icing. However, the icing is not the cake. Before now, it is only children that used to eat the icing. Currently, even children are discouraged from eating it. So, my point is that cake is wholly and fully cake without the icing. In the same way, a marriage is wholly and fully marriage without children.

We need to say this here because many women have been physically and emotionally battered because of childlessness. Because it is the God-given role of a woman to carry a pregnancy and bring forth new life, she takes a lot of flak when she fails to do so after marriage especially in Africa. Most times the trouble starts from the husband. Before long, deliberately or inadvertently, others are brought into the picture. Husband's siblings have often made life unbearable for their brothers' wives and mothers-in-laws have often done worse. This is regardless of the fact that sometimes the fault may not be the wife's. It is a credit to the men that this wife-battering as a result of childlessness rarely comes from fathers-in-law and brothers-in law. Sadly, also women themselves become overwrought when they don't have children especially here in Africa where "a woman is never healthier or happier, becomes more fulfilled than when she makes an outing after confinement". (Love and Health, Ebong Etuk and Udo Etuk p.80)

Going back to our cake analogy, let it be emphasized that cake is fully and completely cake without the icing. Incidentally a beloved brother celebrated his birthday recently with a cake that had no icing. It was beautiful and tasty but the young son was completely perplexed as he asked, "Where is the icing?" I suppose that is how some of us behave when our marriages and those of our loved ones are not immediately blessed with children. We fail to see the love, the togetherness, the removal of loneliness, the food, house, clothes – name it – that go with marriage. All we see is that there is no icing and sometimes we throw tantrums about it. Spouses begin to accuse each other especially if there were events in their past which could lead to childlessness. Others begin to look for non-existent secrets and, especially here in Africa, wives begin to accuse their mothers-in-law of witchcraft. Prayer houses and churches have been built and sustained from revenue accruing from women looking for the fruit of the womb.

The Bible gives us a number of instances of childless marriages and how the couples dealt with the issue. We can learn some useful lessons from them. The first one that quickly comes to mind is that of Abraham and Sarah.

> *"Now Sarai, Abram's wife, had borne him no children. And she had an Egyptian maidservant whose name was Hagar. So, Sarai said to Abram, "See now, the Lord has restrained me from bearing children. Please, go in to my maid; perhaps I shall obtain children by her." And Abram heeded the voice of Sarai. Then Sarai, Abram's wife, took Hagar her maid, the Egyptian, and gave her to her husband Abram to be his wife, after Abram had dwelt ten years in the land of Canaan. So, he went in to Hagar, and she conceived. And when she saw that she had conceived, her mistress became despised in her eyes."*
>
> *- Gen 16:1-5.*

Sarai tried to find a solution for her childlessness using the custom of her day. With the active cooperation of her husband she decided to help God to fulfil His covenant. Though they succeeded in having a child, peace eluded them and has had far reaching consequences that are still being experienced to this day.

Another case in point is that of Hannah and Elkanah. Elkanah went the way of most full-blooded African men. He married a second wife called Penninah. Even though he swore his undying love to Hannah that did not assuage her.

> *'Then Elkanah her husband said to her, "Hannah, why do you weep? Why do you not eat? And why is your heart grieved? Am I not better to you than ten sons?" So, Hannah arose after they had finished eating and drinking in Shiloh. Now Eli the priest was sitting on the seat by the doorpost of the tabernacle of the Lord. And she was in bitterness of soul, and prayed to the Lord and wept in anguish. Then she made a vow and said, "O Lord of hosts, if You will indeed look on the affliction of Your maidservant and remember me, and not forget Your maidservant, but will give Your maidservant a male child, then I will give him to the Lord all the days of his life, and no razor shall come upon his head."'*
>
> *- 1 Sam 1:8-11 NKJV.*

How could she be assuaged when, after pledging his undying love for her he would go and find comfort and children with his other wife and thus exposing her to their taunts? Why would he patronize her with a double portion of food to eat and grow fat and dowdy? If he were more to her than ten sons why did he marry another? I am trying to think like Hannah and enter into her pain which she took to the right court and got her answer. Whereas the husband took the easy, human way out, the wife in her helplessness resorted to God the giver who answered her awesomely.

> *"And the Lord visited Hannah, so that she conceived and bore three sons and two daughters. Meanwhile the child Samuel grew before the Lord".*

> *- 1 Sam 2:21 NKJV.*

So, don't throw your marriage away because there are no children. There are many options today on how to deal with the matter under God.

1. Adoption

    There are many children who have been abandoned by their biological parents. Many were products of unwanted pregnancies. Some are born to teenage mothers who cannot cope with the upbringing of a child. Together the couple can agree to become parents to some of these children. By so doing they satisfy an aspect of the parenting urge and also meet a societal need that is becoming more prevalent on a daily basis.

2. Mentoring

    Some people may not want to go through the legal process of adopting children and giving them their name but they can become role models and mentors to many in the church, school and society. Many children are products of dysfunctional homes and if God brings them your way you can be a surrogate parent. Parenthood is not necessarily a biological function.

3. In-vitro fertilization

    This is becoming a preferred option to those who can afford it. Many of today's 'miracle babies' are actually products of successful in-vitro fertilizations. I believe that it is God that has endowed man with wisdom in this area.

4. Waiting on the Lord

    God still answers prayer like He did in the case of Sarah, Hannah and Manoah's wife.

5. Staying content with each other.

    Let us reiterate the point that a marriage is fully marriage with or without children just as a cake is fully cake without the icing. However, there is beauty, color, attraction in the icing and we pray that God will ice every cake of His children.

Just as we must be careful not to lose our marriages because of childlessness, attention must also be drawn to the fact that the very children that are meant to bless and beautify marriage can turn out to be a blight. That is why the Scriptures admonish:

> *"Train up a child in the way he should go,*
> *And when he is old he will not depart from it."*
>
> *- Prov. 22:6.*

The responsibility for raising a child to become a responsible adult is vested in the two parents. The husband and wife should be seen to be together on all matters concerning their children. As much as possible, they should not show favoritism. A situation where a child runs from the discipline of the father to the coddling arms of the mother (or vice versa) signals a lack of wholesomeness in the marital relationship and will cause the icing to break down, destroying both the icing and the cake.

If you ask God for wisdom on how to raise a child, He will answer you just like He did Manoah.

> *'Then Manoah prayed to the Lord, and said, "O my Lord, please let the Man of God whom You sent come to us again and teach us what we shall do for the child who will be born. And God listened to the voice of Manoah…"' Judg 13:8-9 NKJV.*

Also, there are countless Christian resources on child rearing that are helpful. May the Lord give you discernment in your choices. Whatever you do, do not throw away your marriage because of children – whether they are there or not.

CHAPTER TEN

Finally

This book does not attempt to answer every question about marriage. No book can. The two individuals living the marriage are themselves writing a book that generations after them will read. Even the best and most loving marriages are products of hard work. When we are conscious of the fact that our marriages are speaking of Christ and the church, we will use every resource from the heavenly manual to make them speak well. In this last chapter therefore, we will just lift some Scriptures and songs that you might need to draw from in-between times when you feel the pressures coming.

Gen 1:27-28

So, God created man in His own image; in the image of God He created him; male and female He created them. Then God blessed them, and God said to them, "Be fruitful and multiply; fill the earth and subdue it; have dominion over the fish of the sea, over the birds of the air, and over every living thing that moves on the earth." NKJV

Gen 2:24-25

Therefore, a man shall leave his father and mother and be joined to his wife, and they shall become one flesh. And they were both naked, the man and his wife, and were not ashamed. NKJV

Songs of Solomon 8:6-7

Set me as a seal upon your heart, As a seal upon your arm; For love is as strong as death, Jealousy as cruel as the grave; Its flames are flames of fire, A most vehement flame. Many waters cannot quench love, nor can the floods drown it.

If a man would give for love All the wealth of his house, It would be utterly despised. NKJV

Prov 3:3-4

Let not mercy and truth forsake you; Bind them around your neck, write them on the tablet of your heart, and so find favor and high esteem In the sight of God and man. NKJV

Eph. 4:32

Be kind and compassionate to one another, forgiving each other, just as in Christ God forgave you. NIV

Rom 12:10

Be devoted to one another in brotherly love. Honor one another above yourselves. NIV

Mark 10:6-9

But from the beginning of the creation, God 'made them male and female.' 'For this reason, a man shall leave his father and mother and be joined to his wife, and the two shall become one flesh'; so, then they are no longer two, but one flesh. Therefore, what God has joined together, let not man separate." NKJV

1 Cor. 13:13

But for right now, until that completeness, we have three things to do to lead us toward that consummation: Trust steadily in God, hope unswervingly, love extravagantly. And the best of the three is love. TMB

Eccl. 4:9-12

Two are better than one, because they have a good return for their work:

If one falls down, his friend can help him up. But pity the man who falls and has no one to help him up!

Also, if two lie down together, they will keep warm. But how can one keep warm alone?

Though one may be overpowered, two can defend

themselves. A cord of three strands is not quickly broken. NIV.

1 Peter 4:8

And above all things have fervent love for one another, for "love will cover a multitude of sins." NKJV

GOD, GIVE US CHRISTIAN HOMES

God, give us Christian homes!
Homes where the Bible is loved and taught,
Homes where the Master's will is sought,
Homes crowned with beauty thy love has wrought;
God, give us Christian homes;
God, give us Christian homes!

God, give us Christian homes!
Homes where the father is true and strong,
Homes that are free from the blight of wrong,
Homes that are joyous with love and song;
God, give us Christian homes;
God, give us Christian homes!

God, give us Christian homes!
Homes where the mother in queenly quest,
Strives to show others Thy way is best,
Homes where the Lord is an honored guest;
God, give us Christian homes;
God, give us Christian homes!

God, give us Christian homes!
Homes where the children are led to know,
Christ in His beauty who loves them so,
Homes where the altar fires burn and glow;
God, give us Christian homes;
God, give us Christian homes! AMEN

- (Baptist Hymnal 377)

BIBLIOGRAPHY

Biayebo Edwin, Women, Save Our Men, Enugu, Zero Imagination, 2015.

Blackaby H. and King C., Experiencing God, Ibadan, Baptist Press, 1996.

Chapman Gary, The Five Love Languages, Benin City, Joint Heirs, 2004.

Etuk E. and Etuk U., Love and Health, Lagos, The quantum Company Ltd, 2004.

Heward-Mills, Dag, Model Marriage, Parchment House, 2005

Inyang Udeme, Facebook post of 21/6/2019

La. Haye Tim, How to be Happy Though Married, Illinois, Tyndale House, 1968.

Leman Kevin, Sex Begins in the Kitchen, Grand Rapids, Fleming Revel, 2000.

Oyedele Sam, Marriage and Family Counselling, Ogbomoso, Samak Press and Publishers, 2012.

Oyemomi Emmanuel, Keep Your Marriage Fresh, Lagos, Praise Publications, 2010.

Schlessinger Laura, Woman Power, New York, Harper Collins, 2004.

Templer Richard, The Rules of Love

The Baptist Hymnal, Nigerian Edition, 1995, Ibadan, Baptist Press

THE MESSAGE: The Bible in Contemporary Language © 2002 by Eugene H. Peterson. All rights reserved.)

FCS2178 UNIVERSITY OF Florida Marriage Preep series, Department of Family, youth and Community Science, 2001.

Printed in the United States
by Baker & Taylor Publisher Services